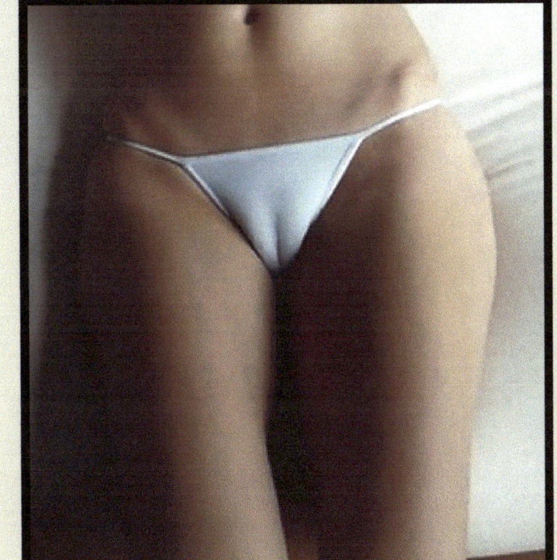

© 2024 Crest Publications Group

Anna Nimity

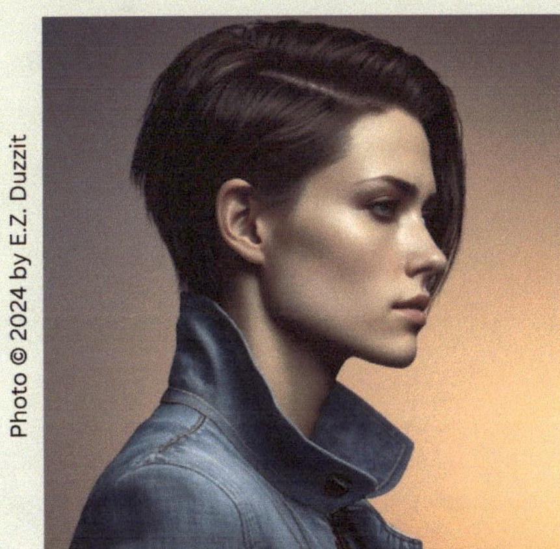

Anna Nimity is just that—undisclosed, unidentified, unnamed, and under an assumed name.

Cover and Interior Design by Maria Tariq

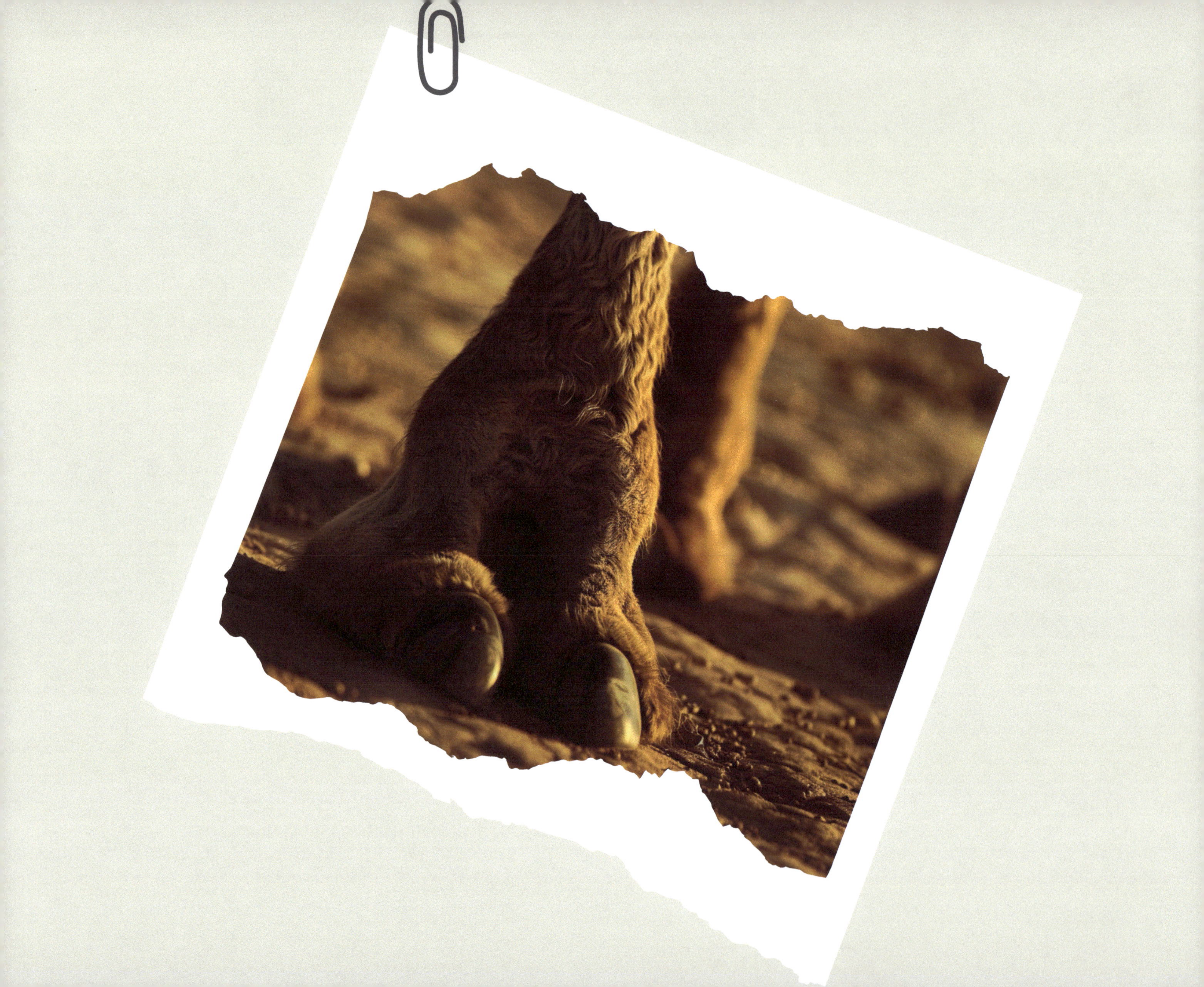

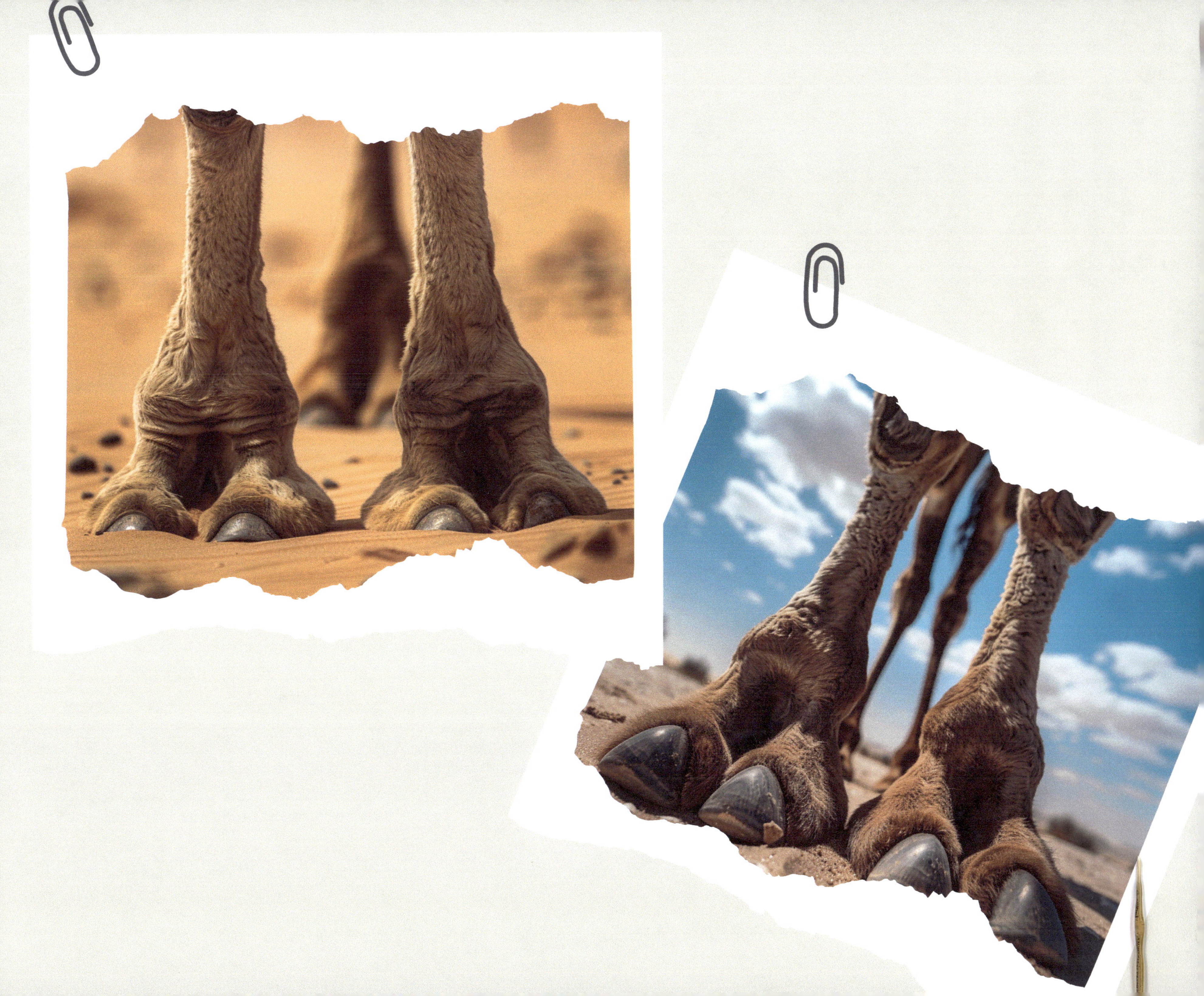

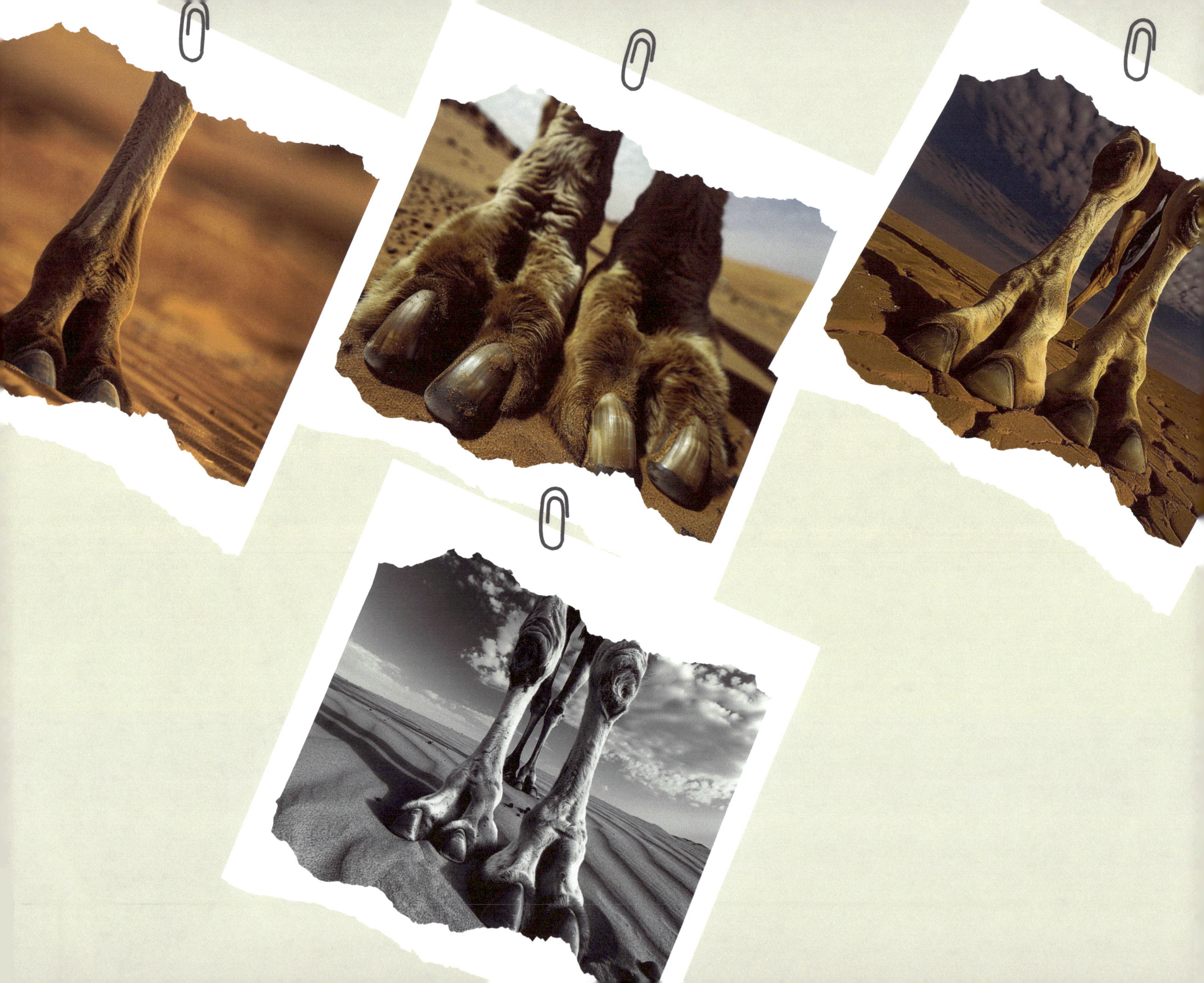

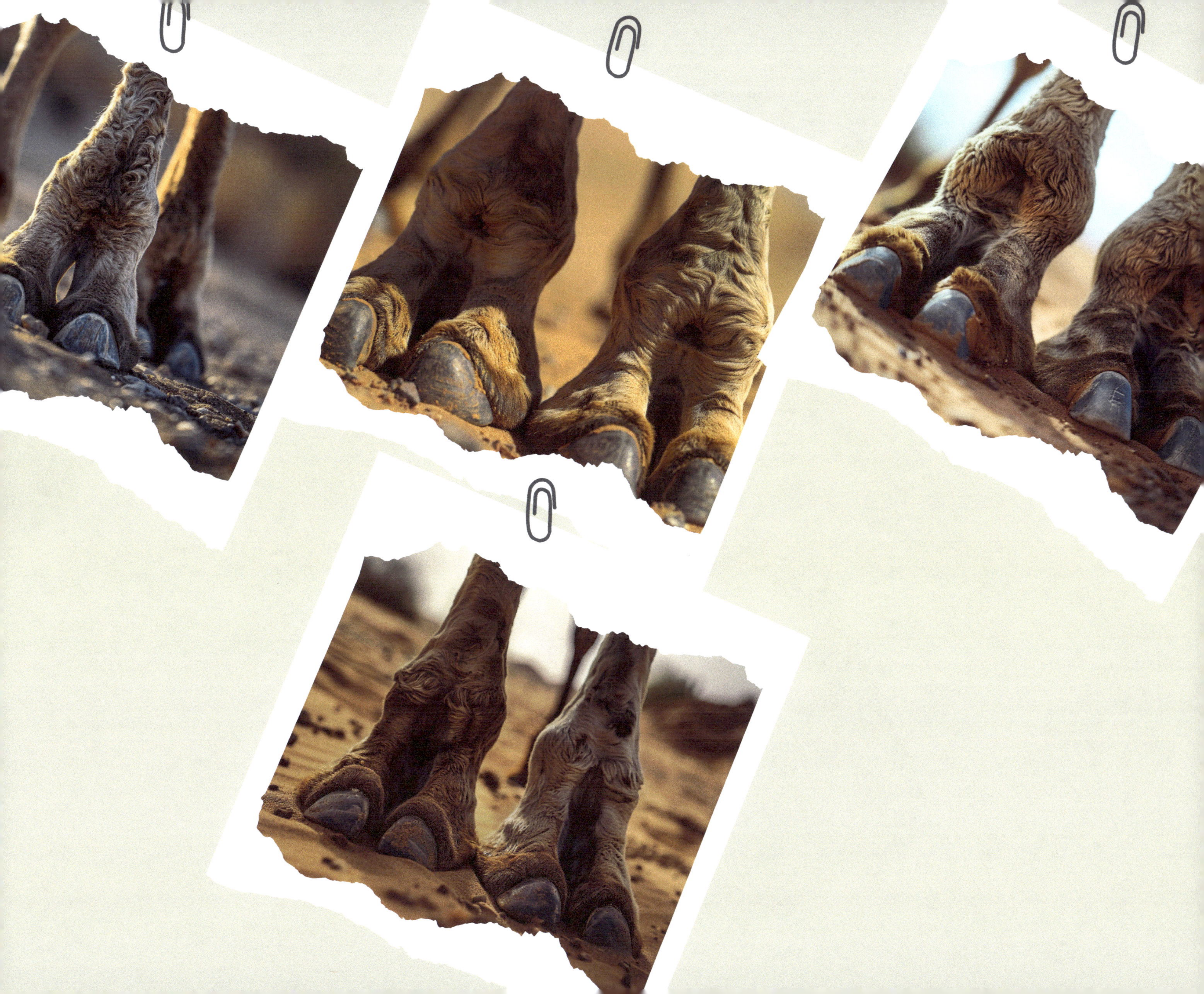

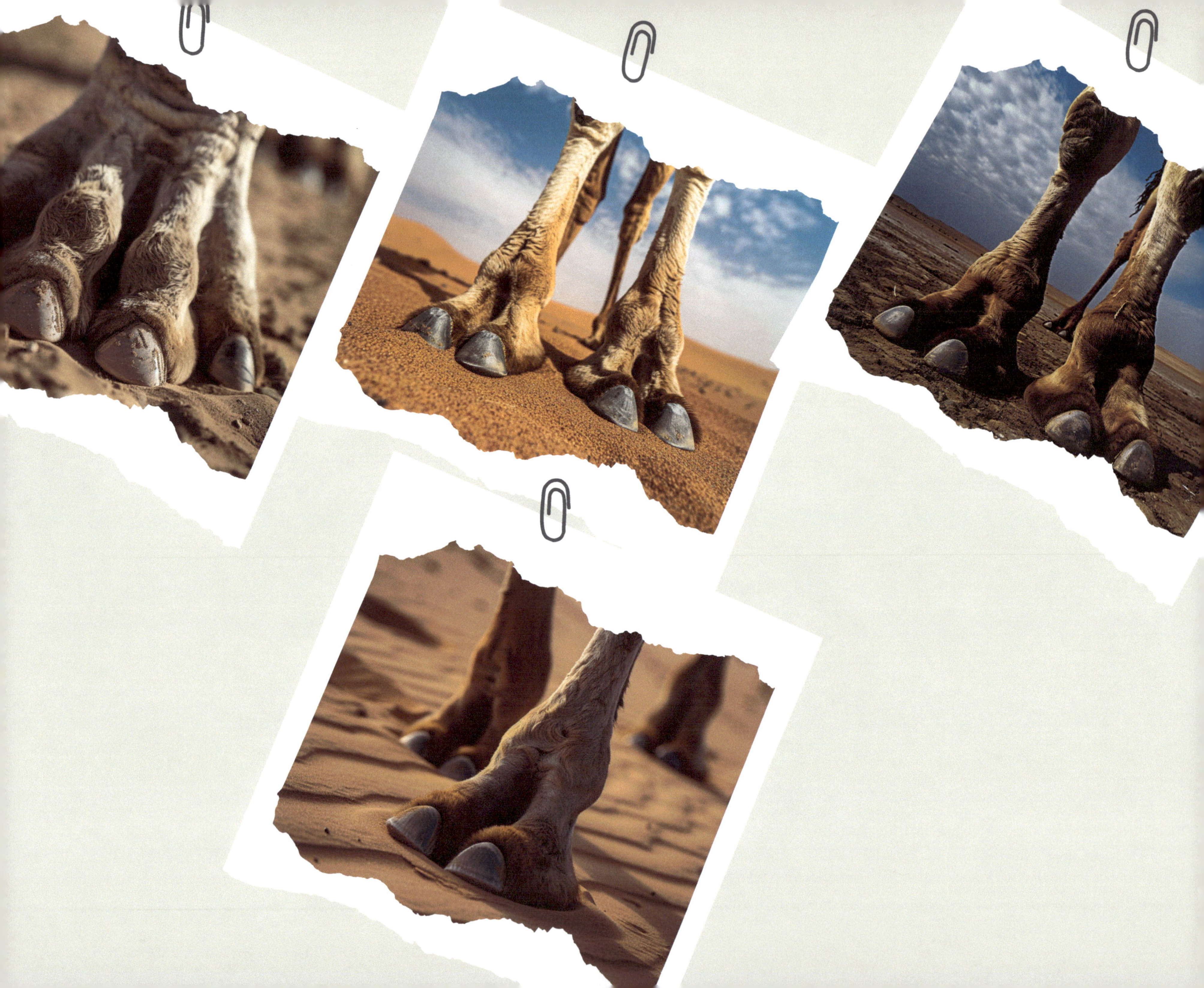

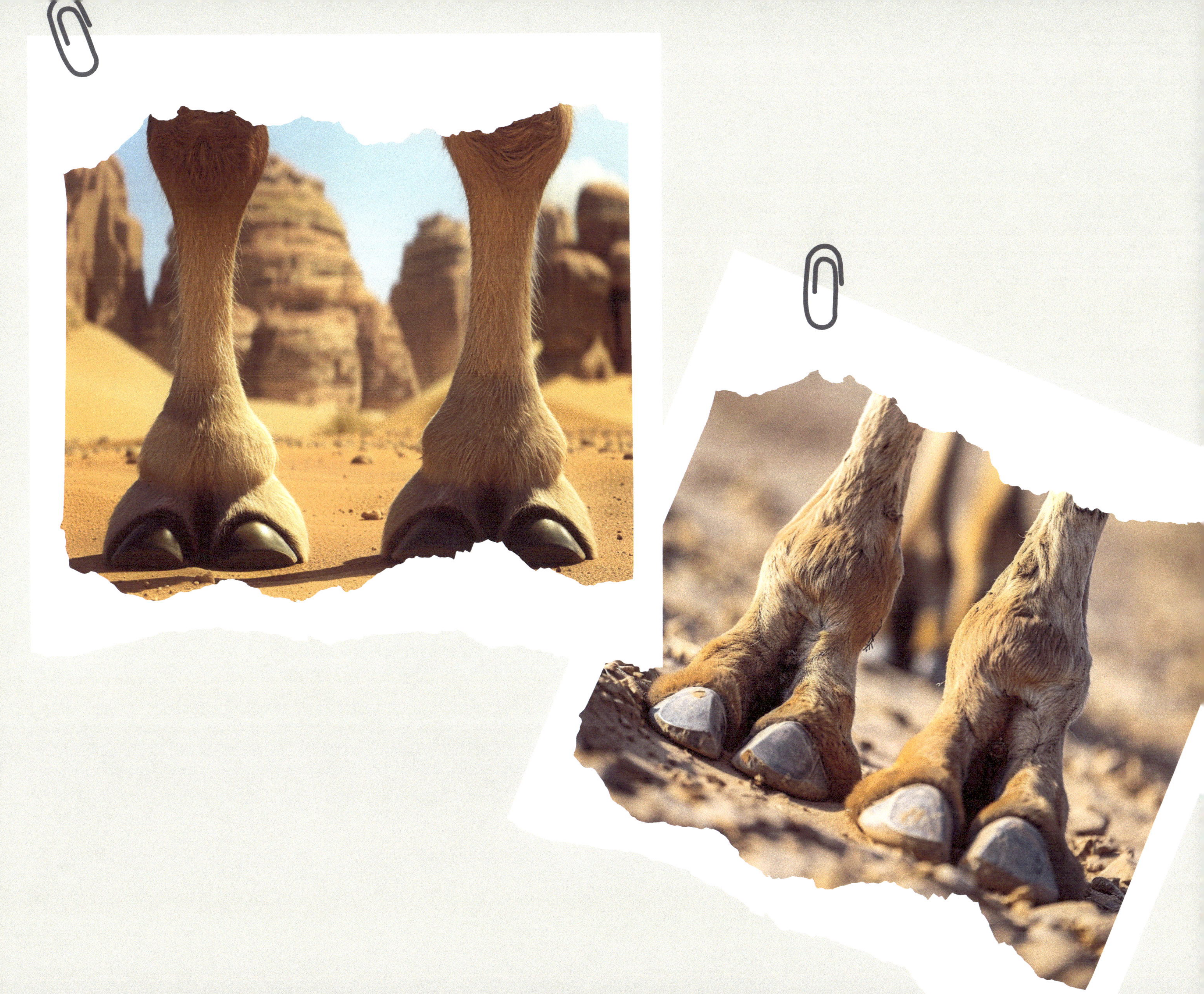

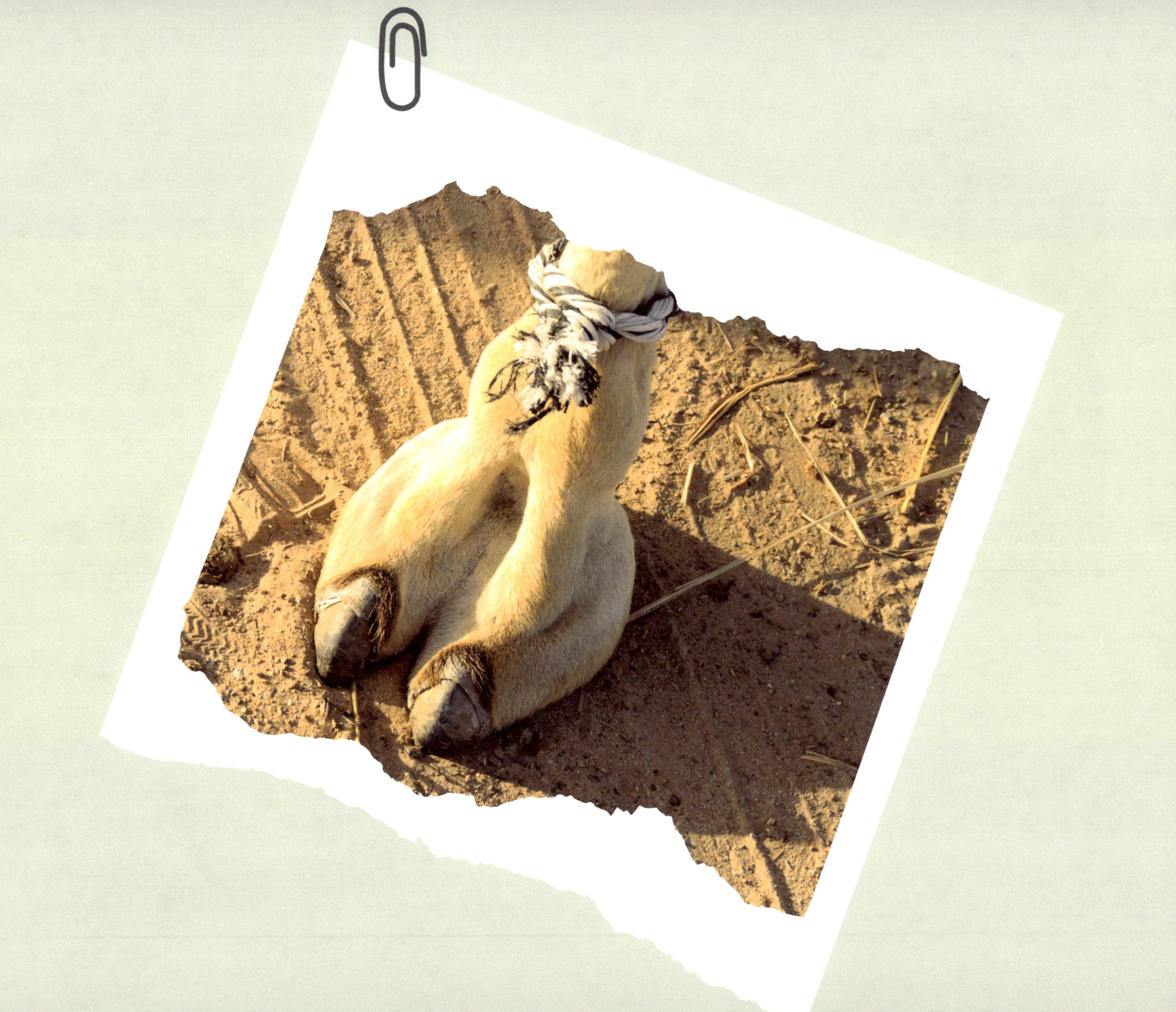

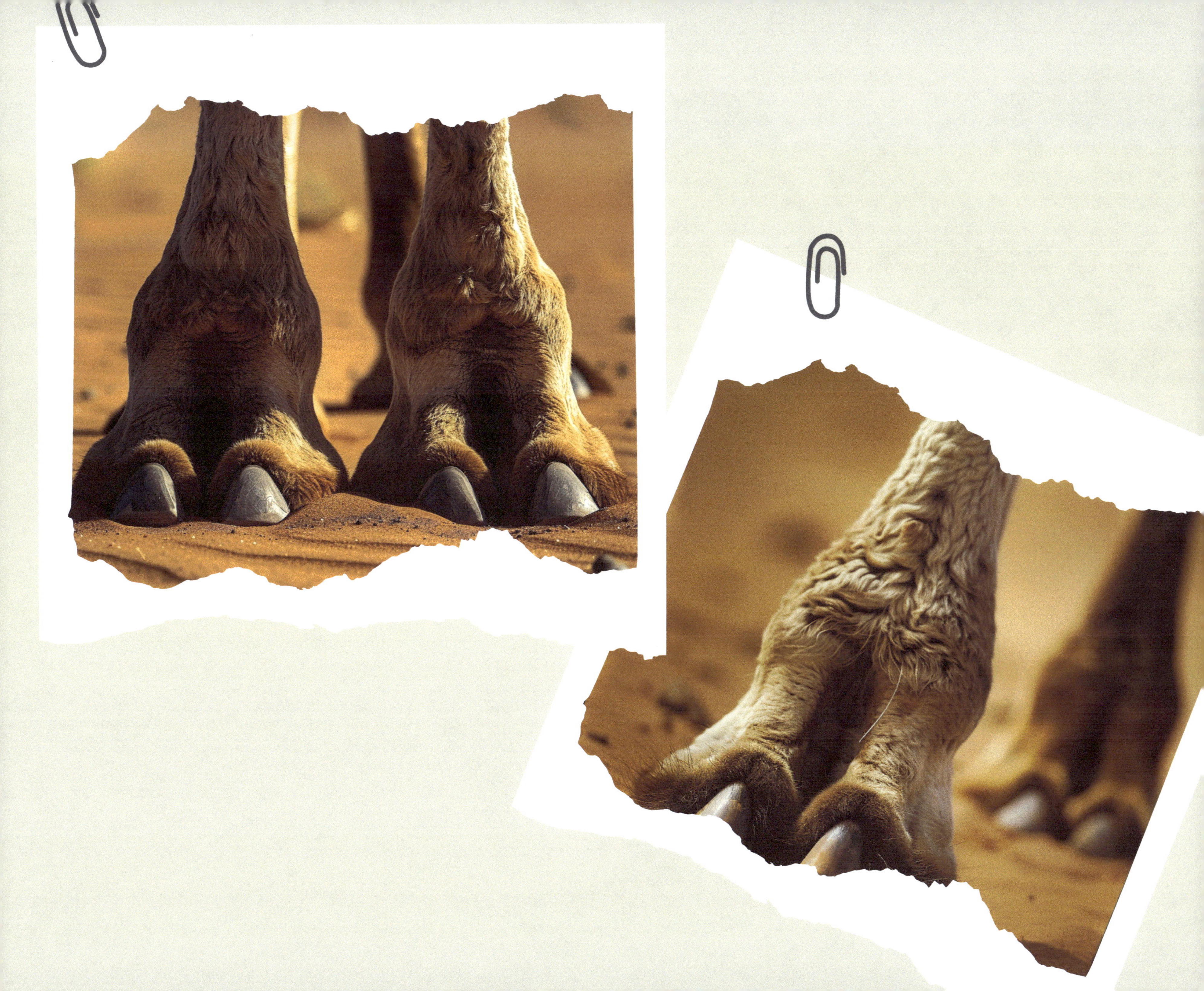

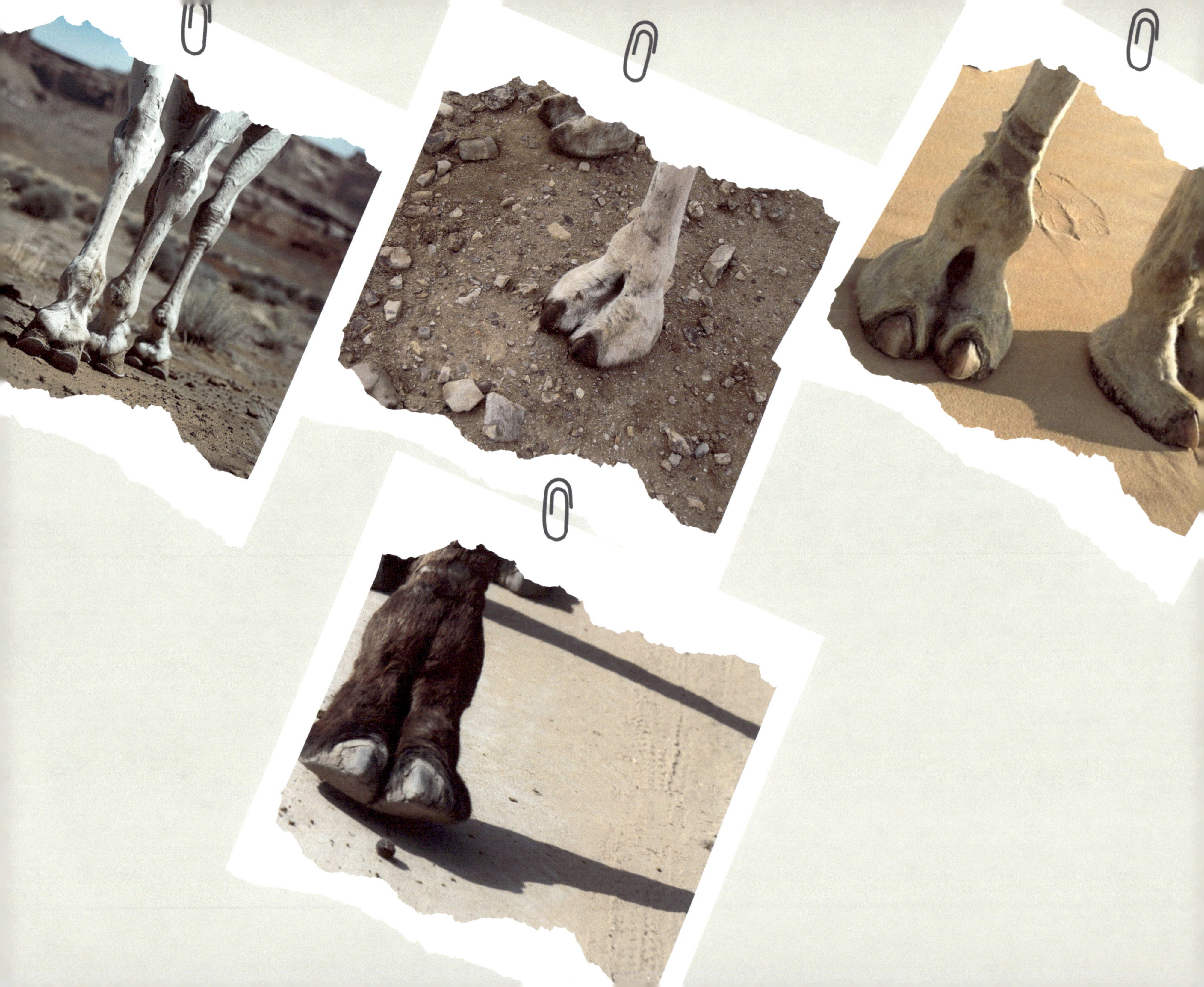

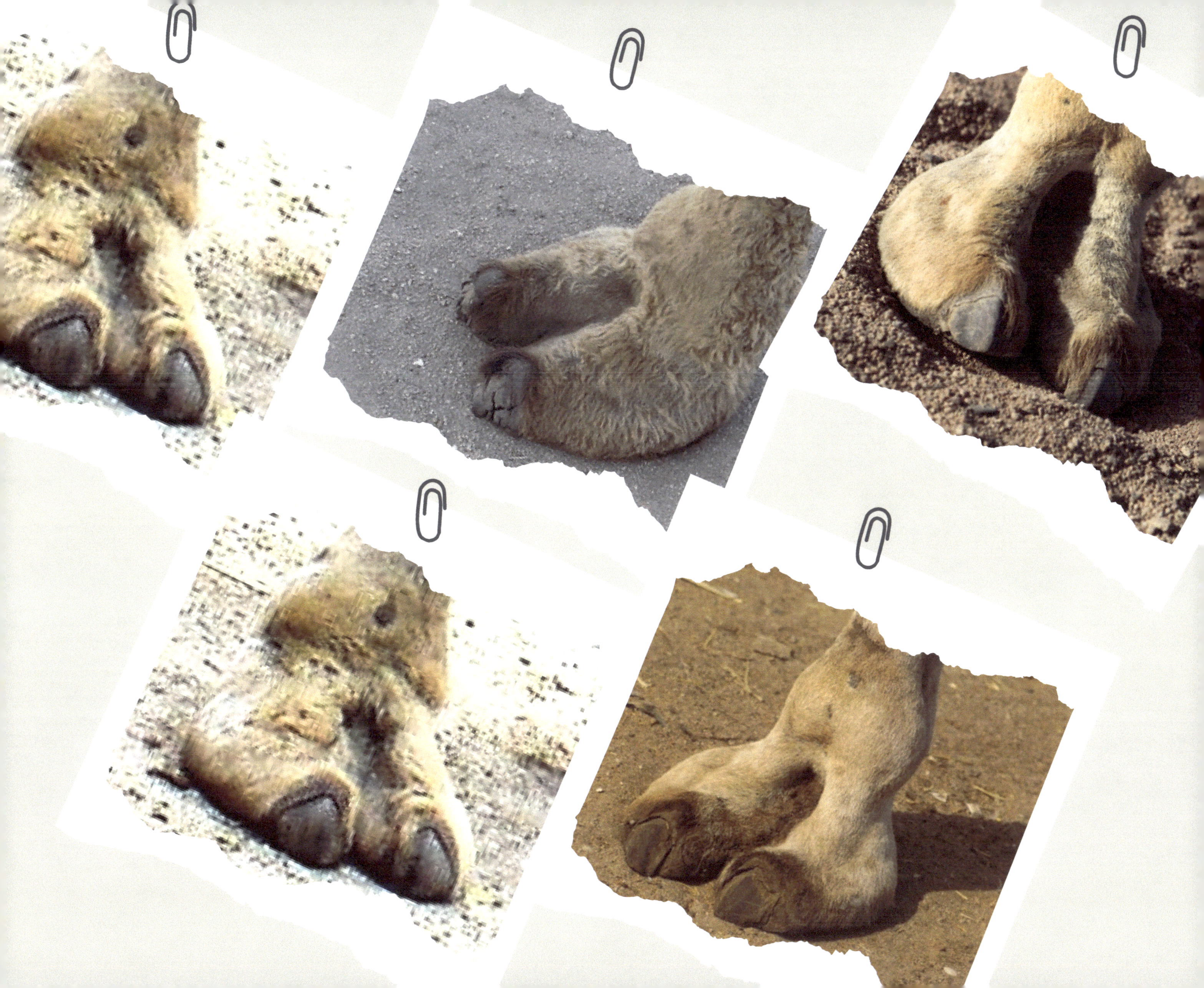

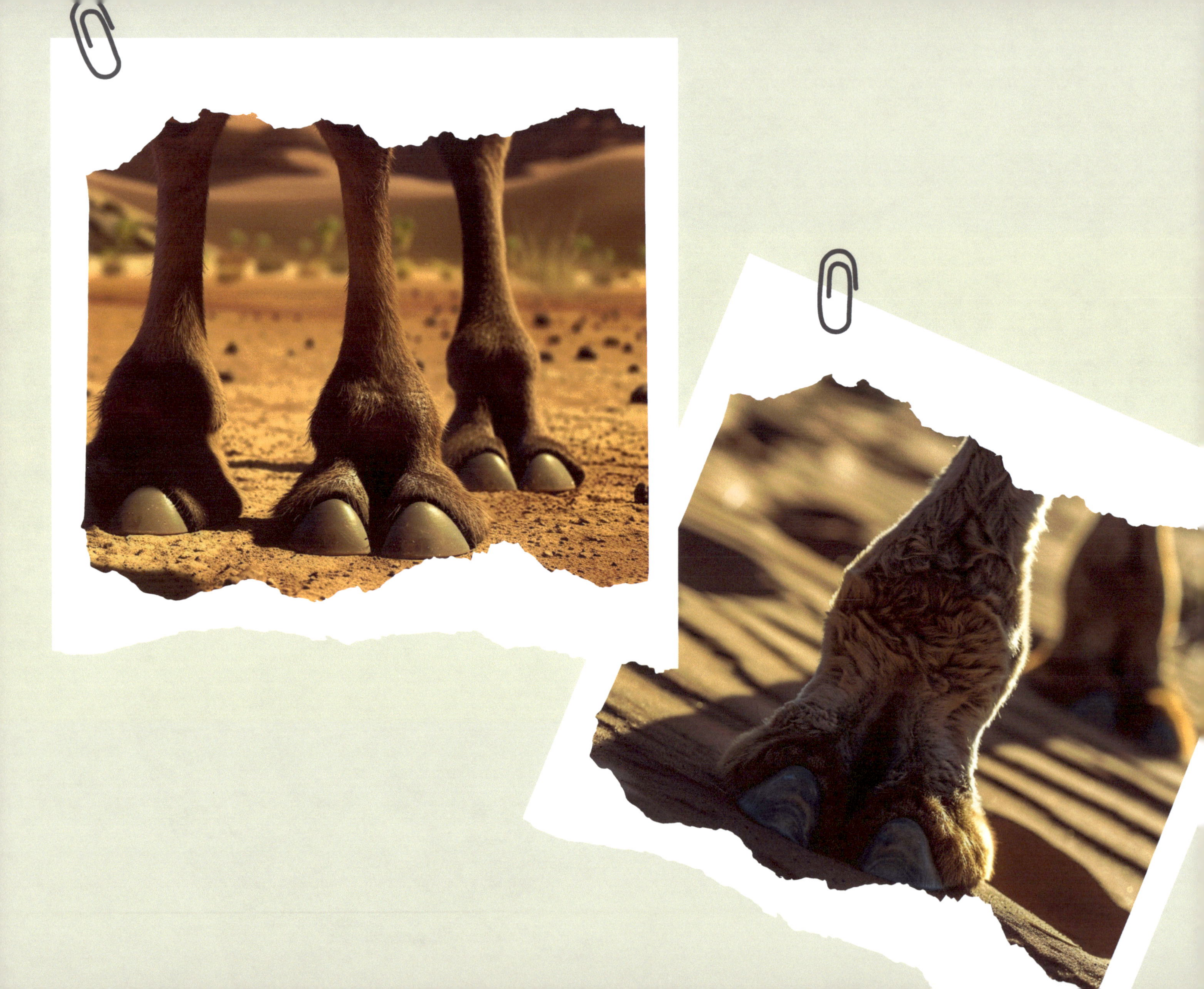

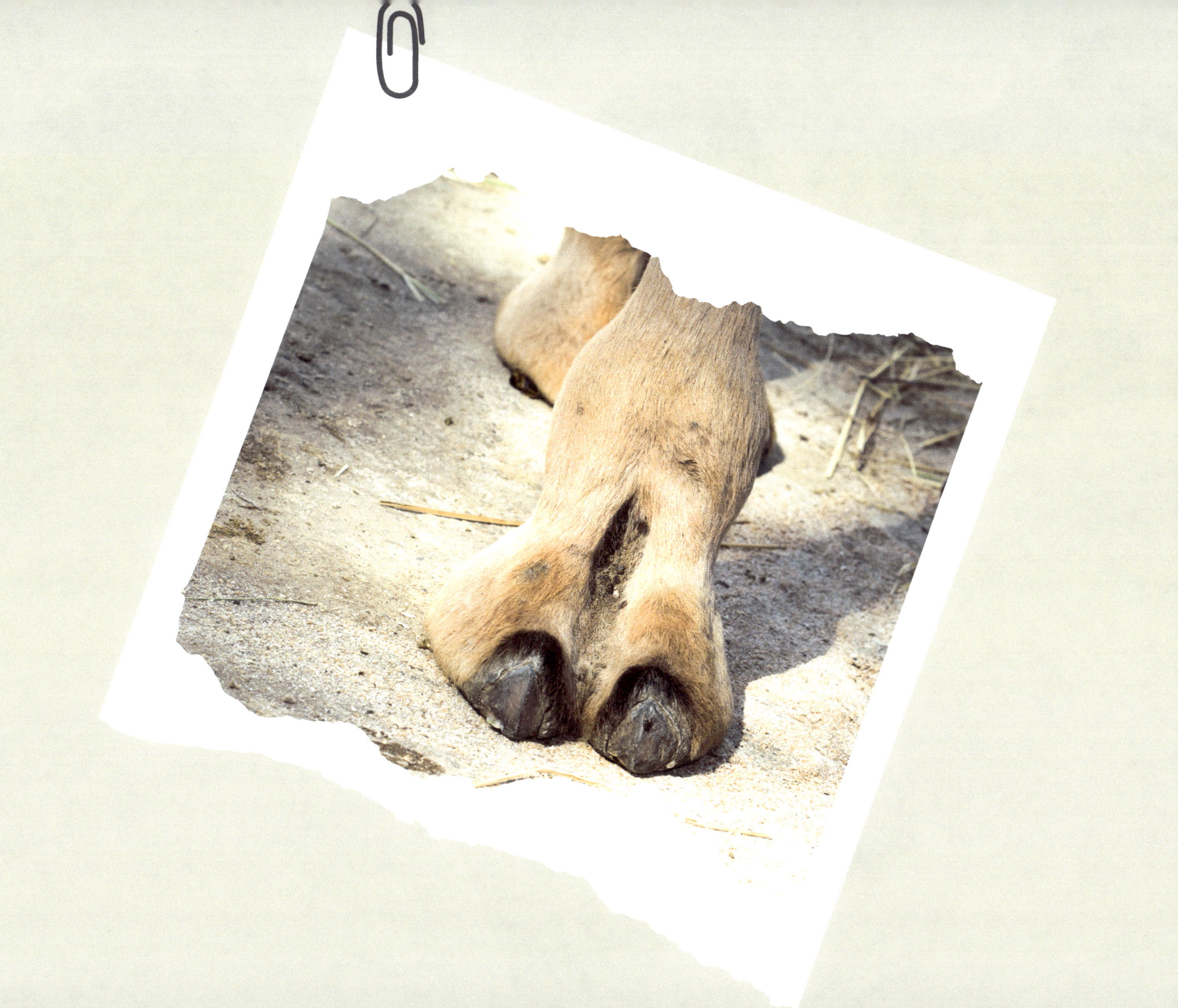

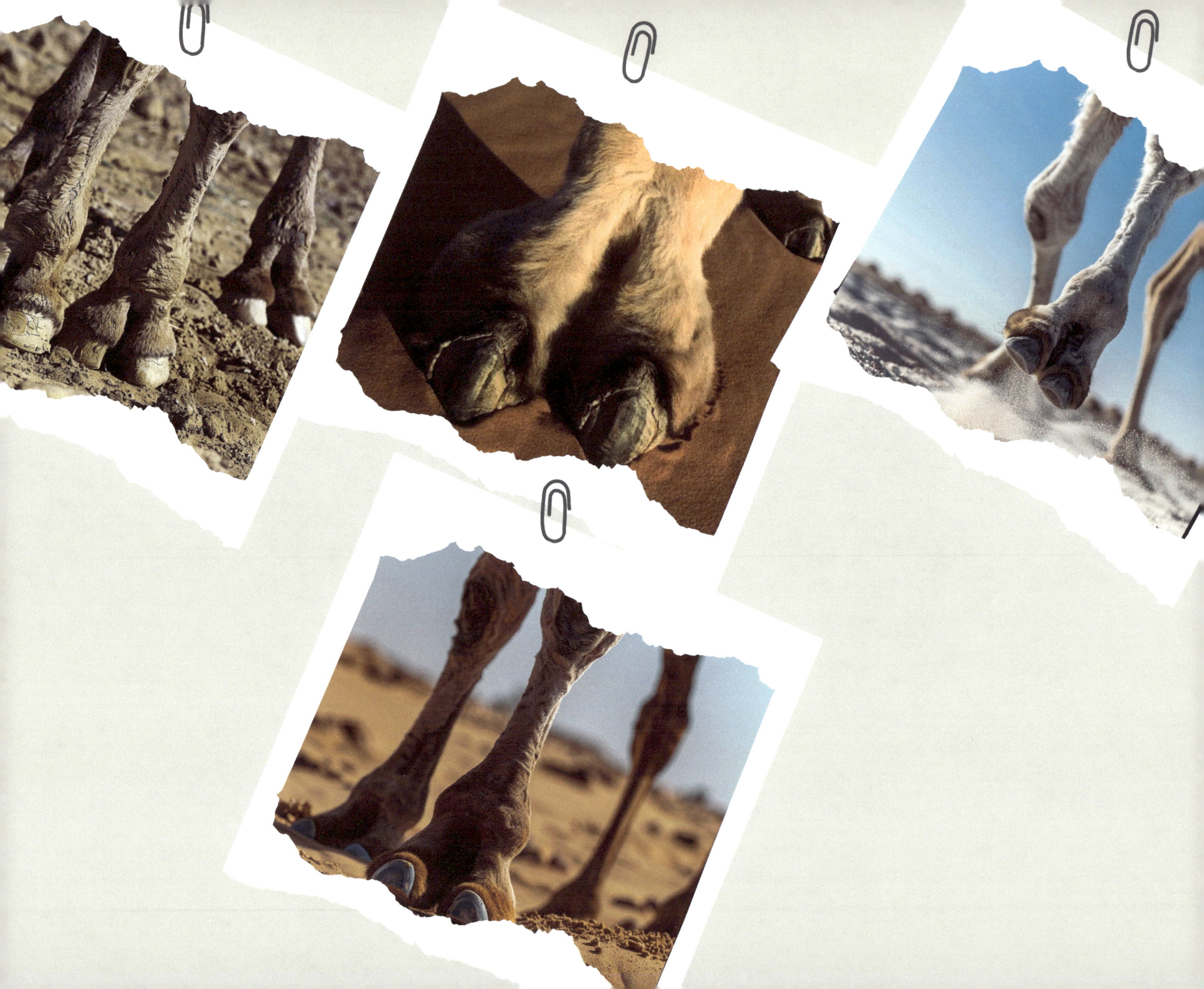

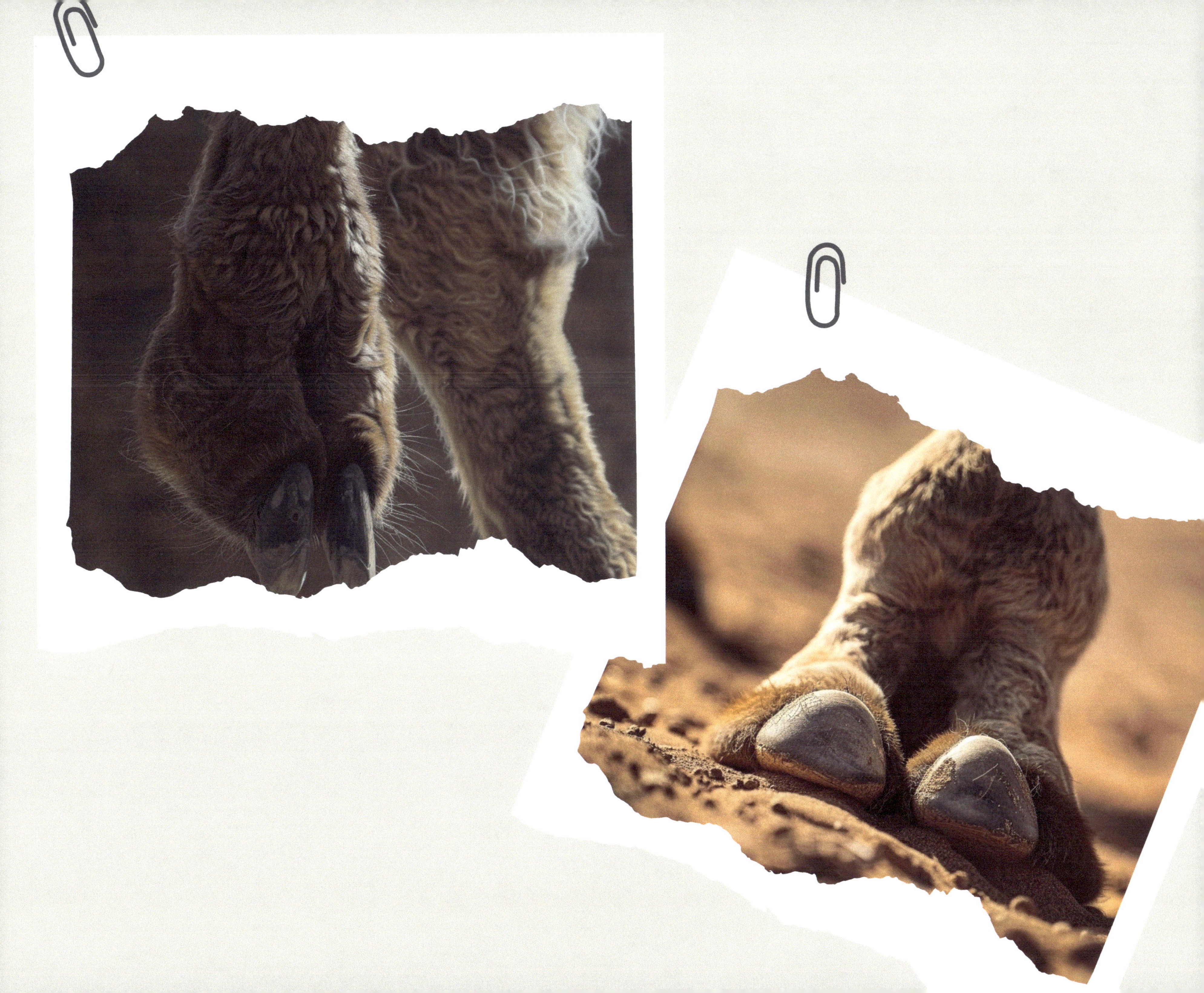

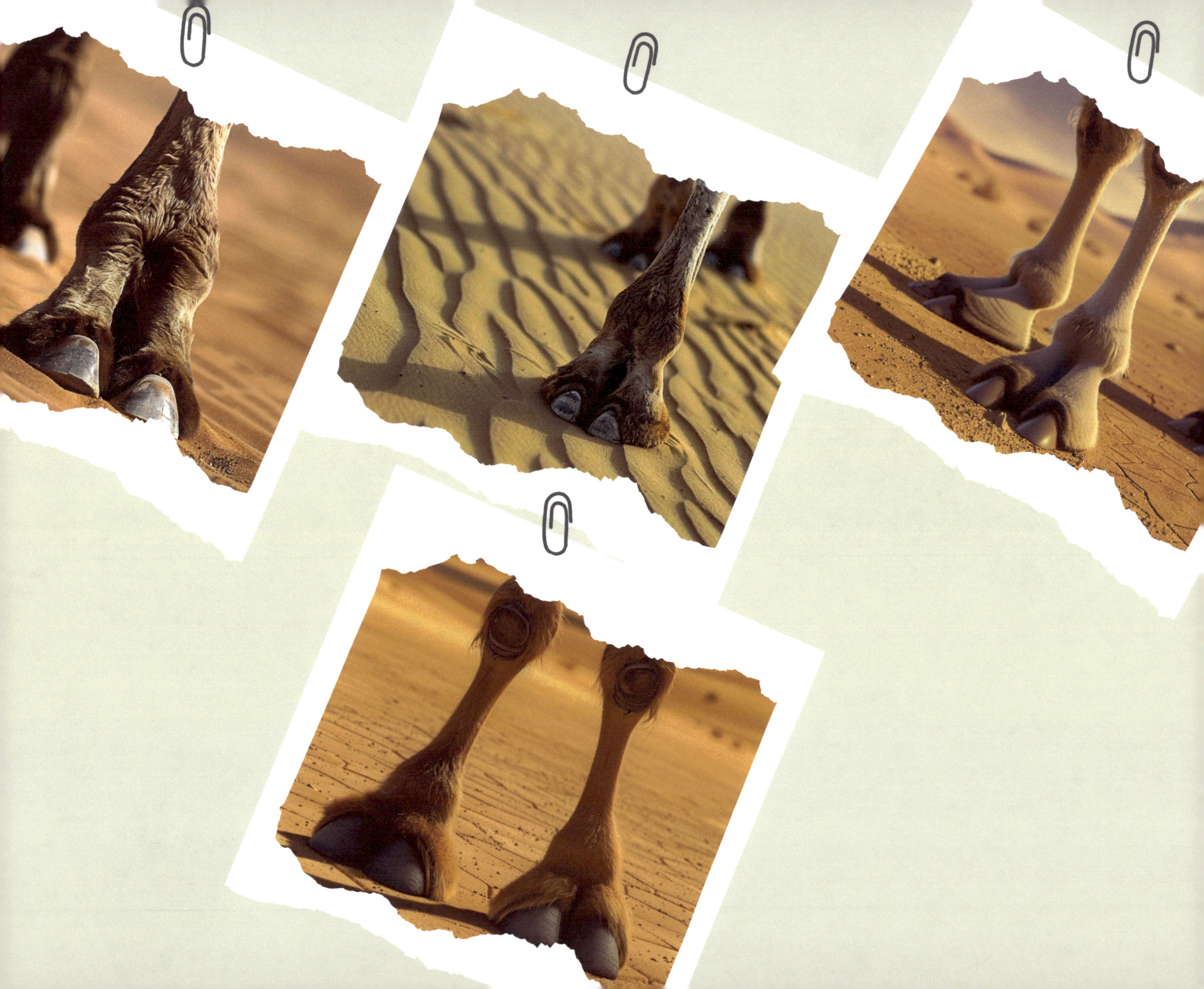

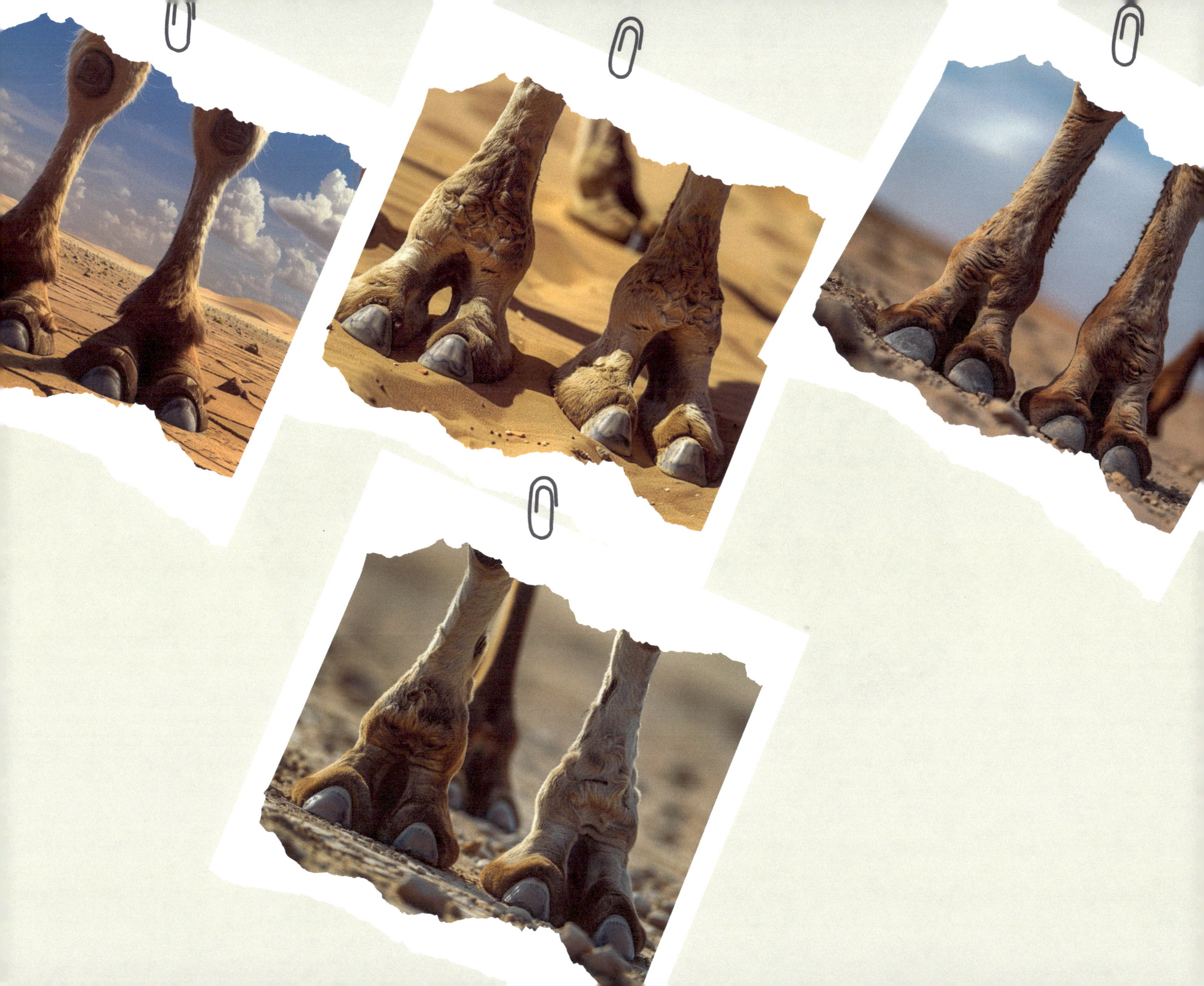

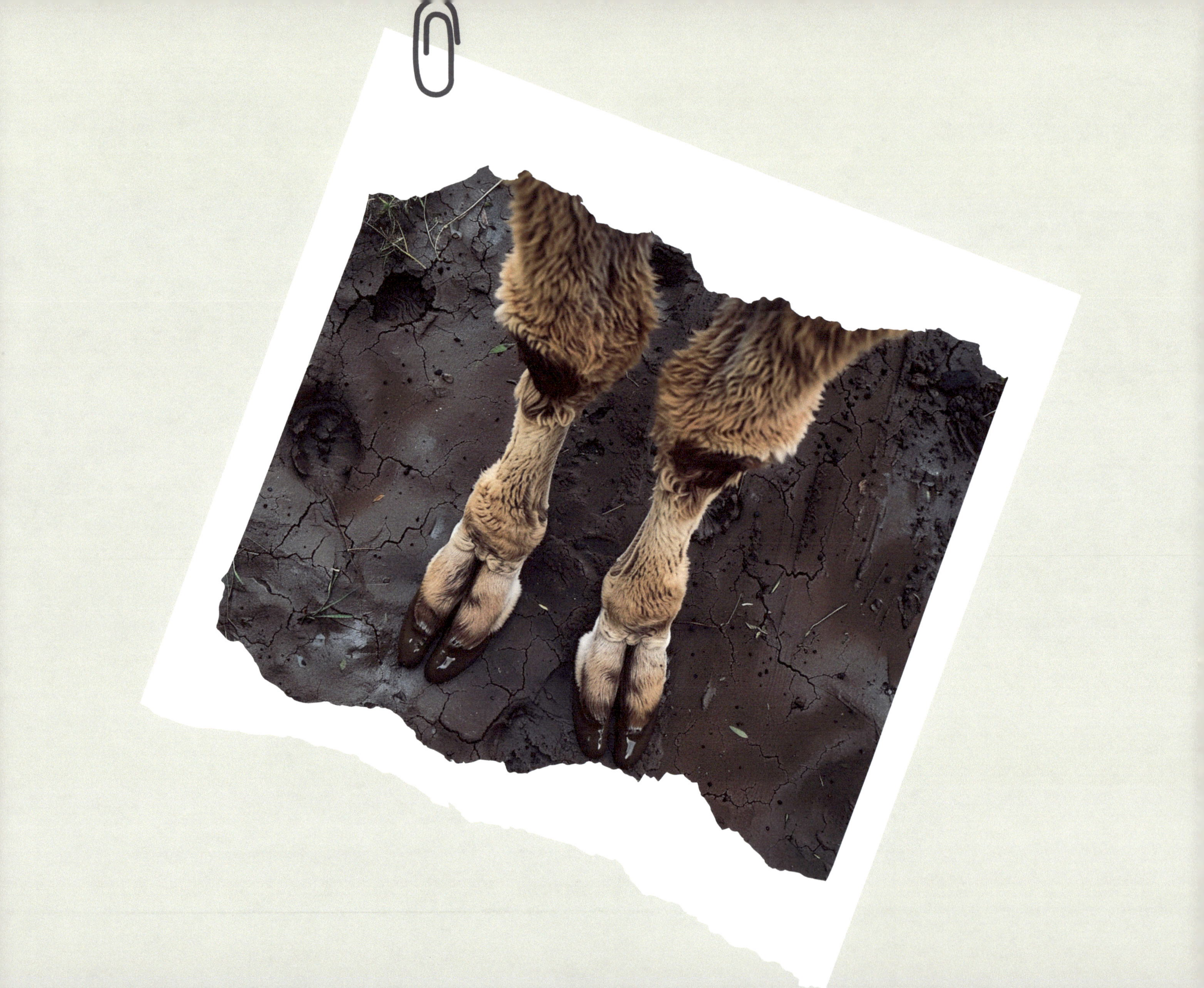

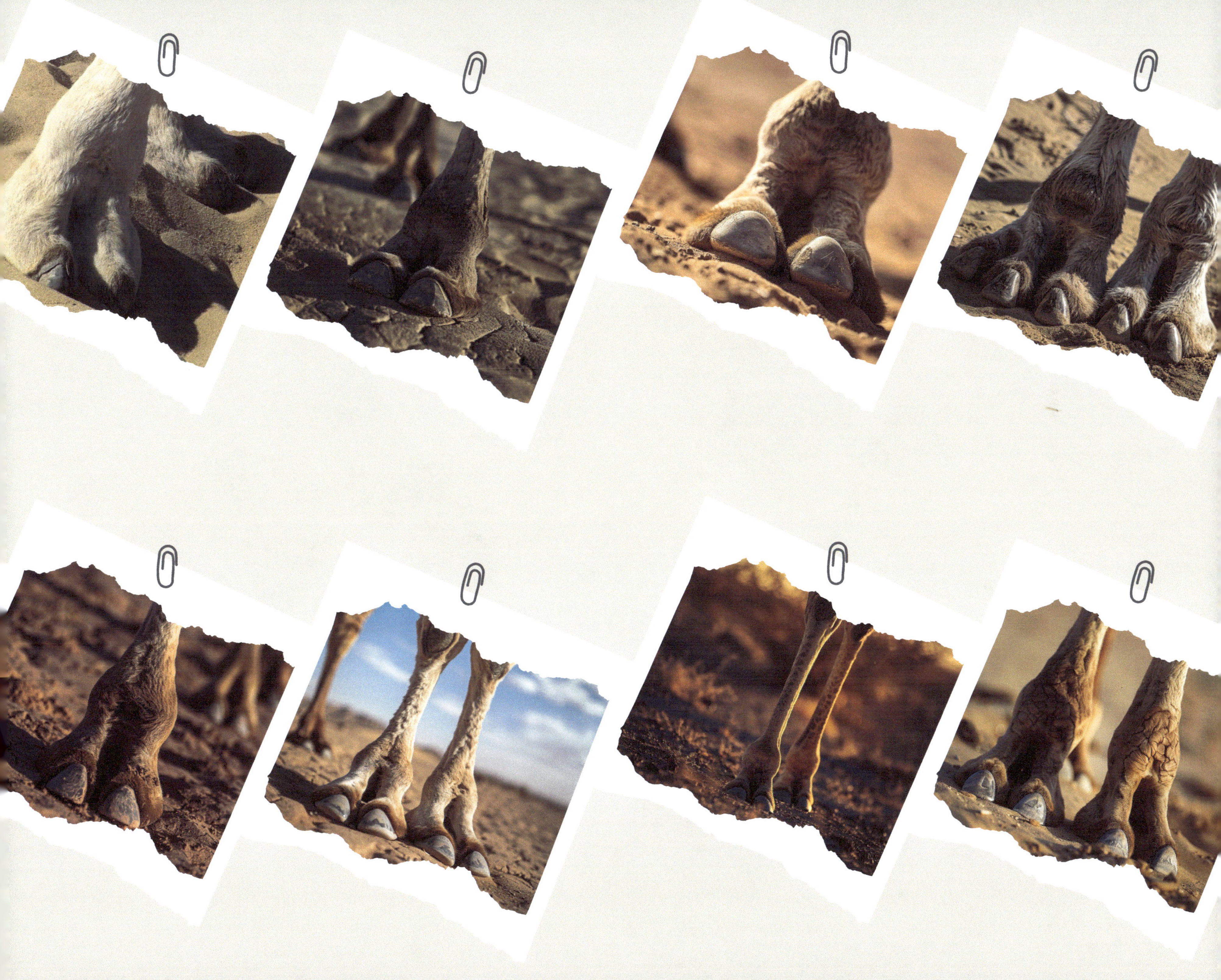

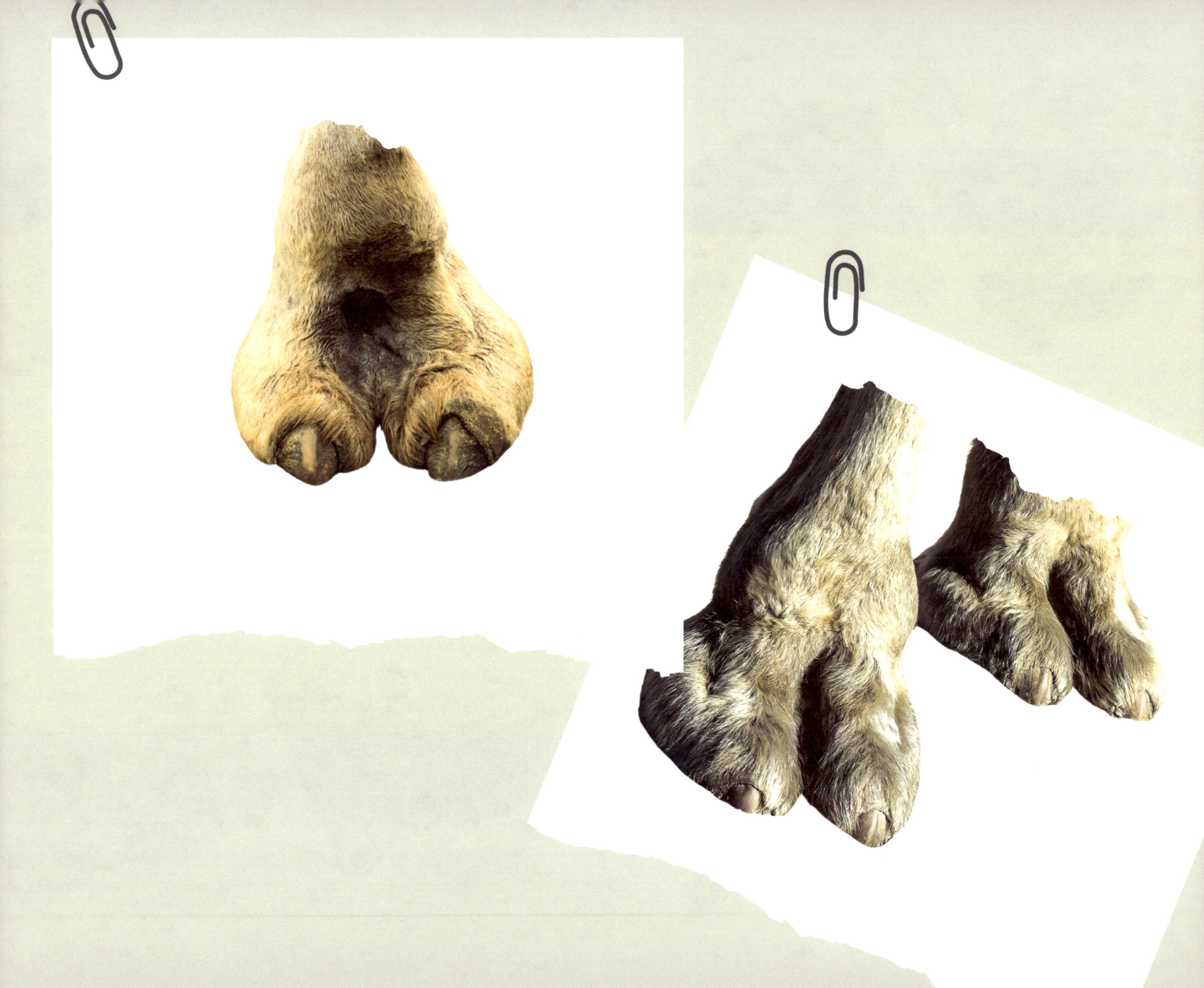

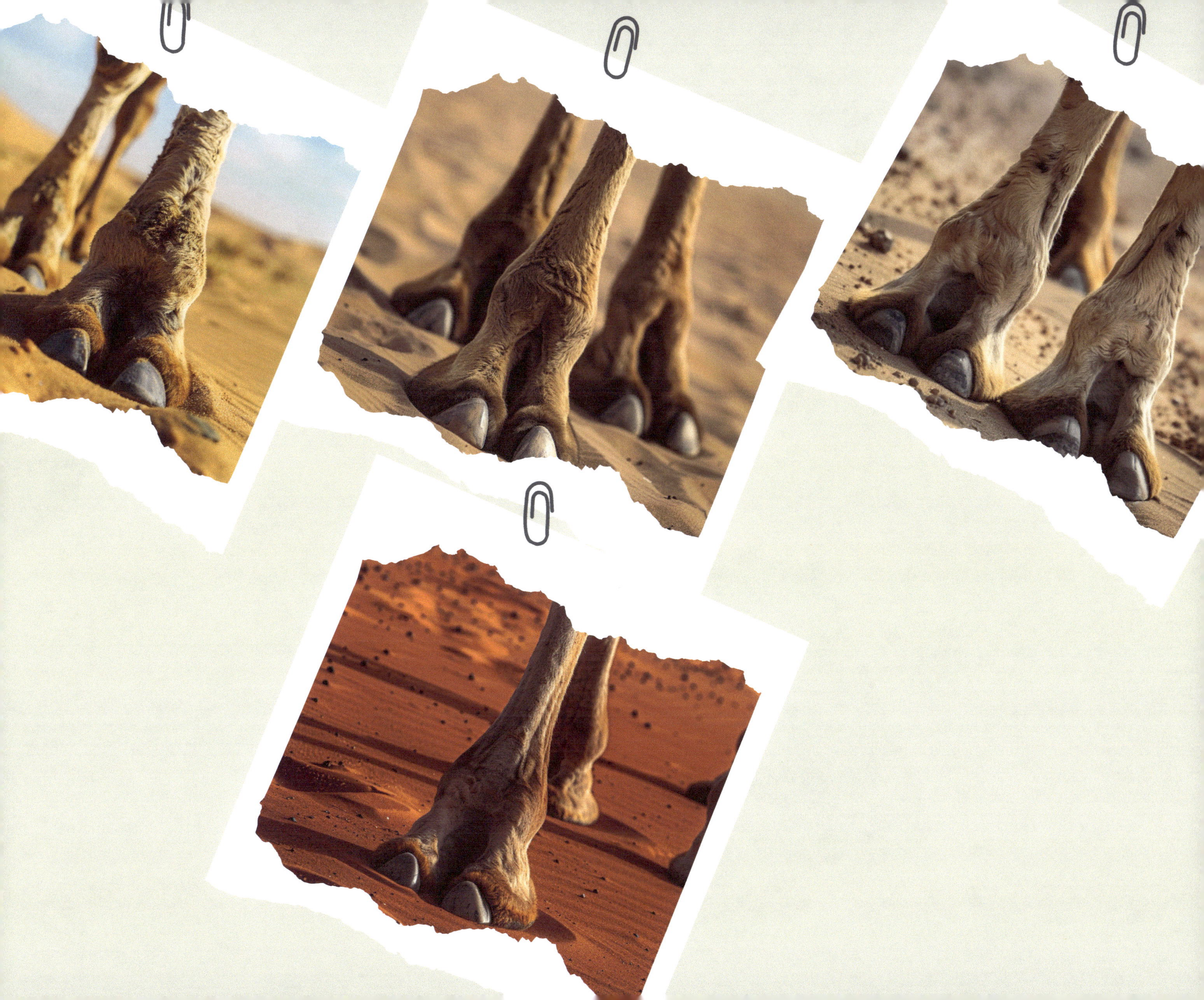

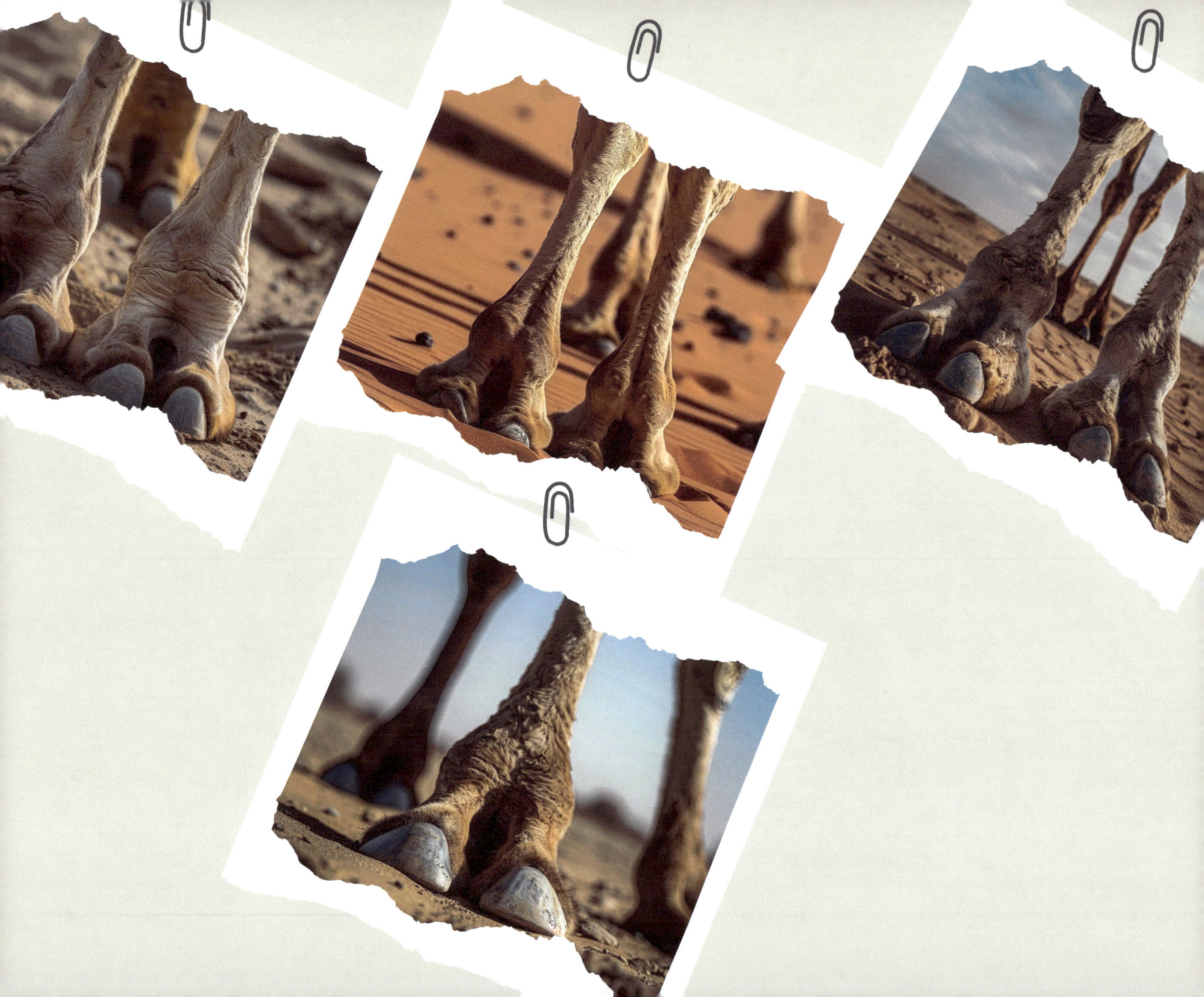

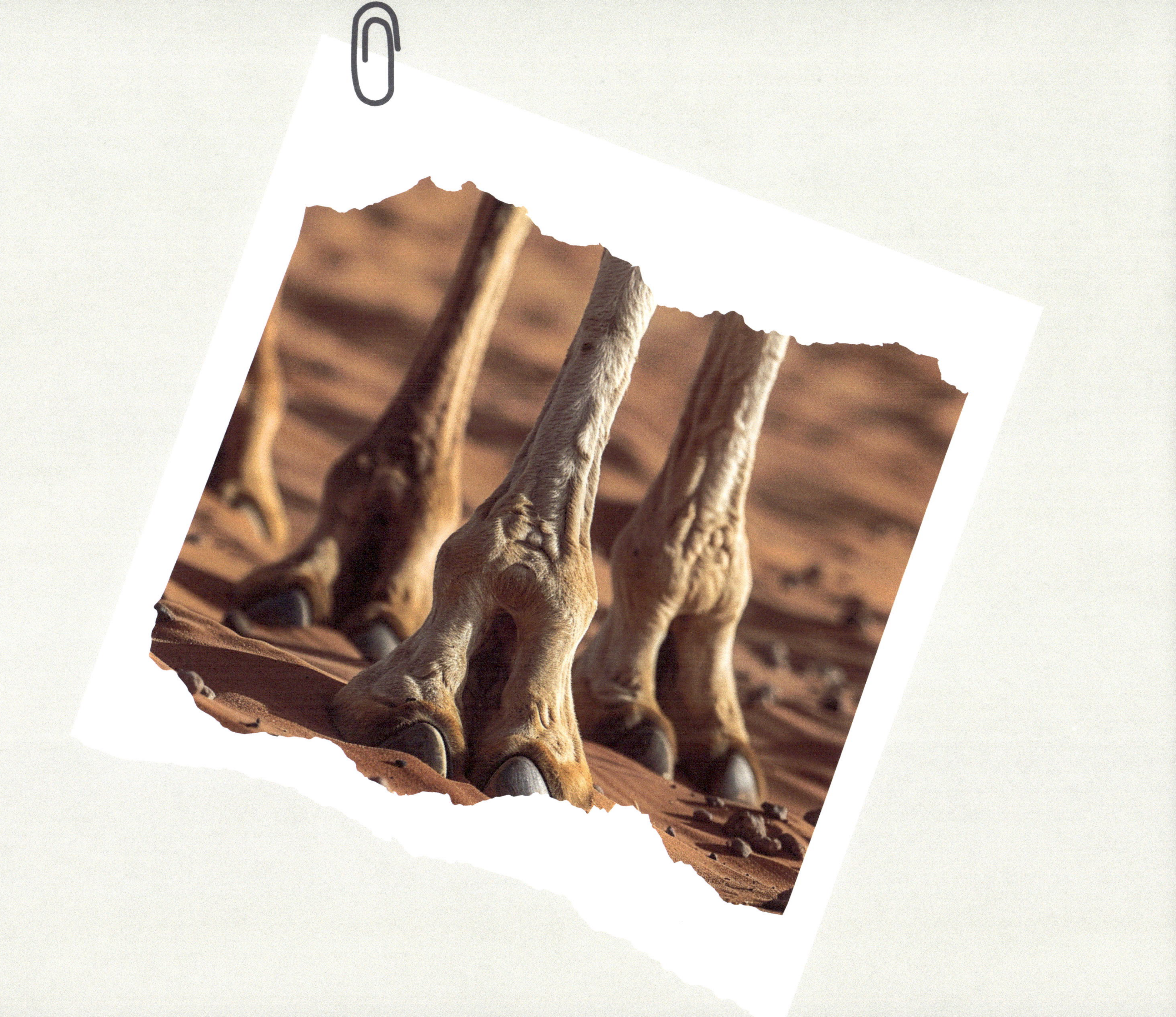

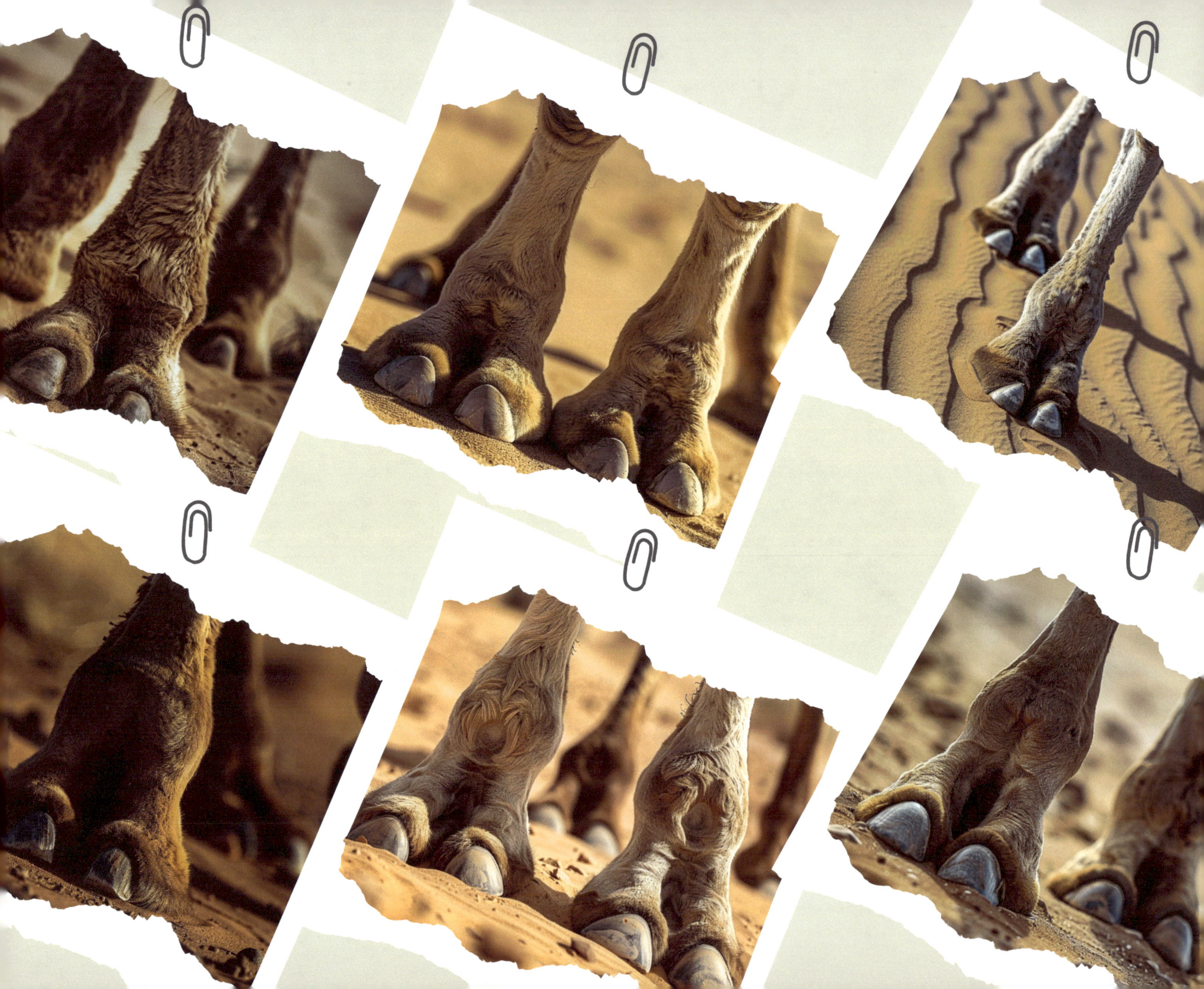